Reflections of a CHILD of the UNIVERSE

ANN MARIE SILVEIRA

DEDICATION

—∞—

This book is dedicated to my dear, departed dad. He was the one who got me thinking about the "good old days" and encouraged me to write about them. He always told me that I could be anything I wanted to be; his love and encouragement have led me to write this book.

TABLE OF CONTENTS

INTRODUCTION

"A human being is a part of a whole called by us 'universe,' a part limited in time and space. He experiences himself, his thoughts and feelings as something separated from the rest, a kind of optical delusion of his consciousness. This delusion is a kind of prison for us, restricting us to our personal desires and to affection for a few persons nearest to us. Our task must be to free ourselves from this prison by widening our circle of compassion to embrace all living creatures and the whole of nature in its beauty."
—Albert Einstein

The past is a powerful force filled with stories and memories. Childhood especially is a magical time, as well as a reference for the rest of our lives. Everyone sees the world differently. A child's view is the most imaginative and may surprise adults. Let's take a look at everyday life through a child's eye growing up on a family farm, and you will laugh throughout! As the child grows, I bet you will be surprised at your reactions and memories of your own experiences.

I hope you enjoy my book.
Ann Marie

CHAPTER 1

A CHILD'S VIEW OF THE WORLD

ON THE FARM

Grass as far as you can see. As an adult, seventeen acres is quite a bit of land, but as a child it was much more to me; it was my whole world!

I loved the outdoors – lying in the grass, listening to the pigs oink in glee as they squished around in the mud after a good rain, and watching the nanny goat play with her baby. Because there were five big, beautiful dogs on the property, I could never go very far on my own. It was as if they had been charged to watch over me and take care of me.

Vividly I remember once tripping over a rock, daydreaming as usual, and when I fell, I skinned my knees badly. Bleeding and in shock, I sat down on the grass and started to cry. Immediately four of the dogs sat down around me and started to lick my face. The fifth dog, a huge German shepherd, ran to the farmhouse and let everyone know of my plight. Within minutes, my grandmother ran out to comfort me. She brought me inside the farmhouse, bandaged my knees and gave me two of her wonderful, homemade oatmeal cookies with a huge glass of milk. It was ALMOST worth the fall!

THE COAL STOVE

I loved to sit in front of our coal stove in the kitchen, my little chair pulled up as far as I could get to it without burning myself. The heat felt so good on my face, I could sit there for hours. My parents thought this was strange and were always trying to get me to do something else, especially on rainy days. But I usually managed to get my way!

MOM AND LEMONS

Mom always washed her jewelry in lemon juice and water. She said it made them very shiny. I didn't have any jewelry, but I loved the smell of the lemons. I decided that when I grew up and had jewelry, I would also wash them in lemon juice and water to make them shiny.

BEST DAY OF MY LIFE

Mom and me, the wind blowing softly, ocean waves lapping at my toes, seagulls flying, sand castle completed, a cold soda in my hand. Sun shining, not a cloud in the sky, children laughing, the smell of hot dogs and sunscreen in the air. Surfers cutting through the waves, their boards shiny and slick; huge waves rolling in and breaking on the shore. Best day of my life!

THE BARN

One day it was my castle, the next day the beach. It was whatever and wherever I wanted it to be! The huge pile of coal in the corner was the evil mountain, the tractor was my horse, and the many cats that lived in the barn were all my friends. I draped a large towel over the table so it would keep the rain off my fort underneath. I had picked some wildflowers in the field, and I lined these up in the pan and used them to make a delicious dinner for me and the cats. Then we washed it all down with a bottle of milk I had taken from the kitchen. The barn was also a great place for a nap, and I cuddled with the animals until it was time for dinner.

THE POTATO CELLAR

When it was very hot outside and in the barn, I had another secret hiding place. There was a cellar in grandpa's farmhouse; part of it had a dirt floor, and it was very cold in there. That was his potato cellar. Grandpa grew a lot of potatoes and he wanted us to be able to eat them all year, so when the potatoes were ready, he harvested them from the garden and put them in the potato cellar. They never went bad in there and we could cook and eat them whenever we wanted to!

SEWING

I decided early on that I would have the best-dressed dolls in town. It was easy because Grandma knew how to sew and she was my best friend. I had lots of doll dresses to choose from – one for every day of the week. She sewed my clothes too, beautiful dresses and pants. And then there were the pillow cases... Grandma told me she washed the bags the chicken seed had been stored in and made pillows for all of us to sleep on. I asked Grandma if the chickens had pillows too, but she just laughed.

GRANDPA'S RESTAURANT AND BAR

How cool it was to know that there was a party down-stairs every night! I hid on the stairs, peeking through the railing, watching all the dressed-up ladies flirt with the Navy sailors. Maybe someday I could get one of those white caps they wore for myself.

GRANDPA'S MEDICINE

Grandpa used everything that grew on his farm, and using plants and herbs to relieve pain was no excep-tion. I was too young at the time to remember all the poultices and teas he made for us when we were not feeling well, but I remember a few. He soaked chamomile and dandelions in boiling water and then strained the liquid. We were told to drink the tea for an upset stomach. It helped!

Grandpa also had a lot of purple (my favorite color) African violets inside his farmhouse. They were very pretty, but I once asked him why he had so many. He said they bring inner peace and happiness to anyone who lives there. Well, that was true; I was very happy living on the farm!

Grandpa also made cinnamon tea often. When I asked him why, he said it helped lower his blood pressure. Worried, I asked him if I had caused his high blood pressure. He just laughed and said no.

DOLLS

I have collected dolls since as far back as I can remember. One of my very first dolls when I was small was made out of sawdust and cloth. I loved that doll, but one day her stuffing started to spill out through a small hole in the cloth. I thought that she was dying. What a relief that Grandma was able to sew her back together. She made my doll live for many more years!

WISDOM

Wisdom was not something that was lost on me, even at an early age. I figured out that most people would not think that growing up on a farm was a big deal, but they were so wrong! I truly believe that if every child spent two years on a farm, our civilization would change, and our country would be a better place. The interaction and closeness one experiences with the animals on a farm every day is not something a city girl could even begin to understand. I learned respect, patience, what it means to be a friend, and how life could be so cruel at the same time, all by watching the animals on my grandpa's farm.

BITING MY NAILS

We had a neighbor lady, Grandma's friend, who came over often for tea. She had a habit of biting her nails, so I started to do the same. Then I started getting sick quite a bit, and Grandma said that if I stopped biting my nails, I wouldn't get sick so often. Well, my grandmother was very smart, and she was right!

MY FAVORITE HOLIDAY

Christmas, of course! I firmly believed that Santa Claus would bring lots of gifts if you were good and a lump of coal if you were not. I always made sure that Santa knew what I wanted in advance so he had plenty of time to get my gifts – and I tried my best to be good!

ANGELS

Pretty pictures in books. I loved their wings and wished I could fly! They all lived in heaven and visited us from time to time. When they visited, I firmly believed, they became guardian angels and helped us with whatever they could.

MY DAD

I loved my dad and he loved me. He has always been my hero. He was a pilot before I was born, and he knew how to fix anything. I decided that when I grew up, I would marry someone like him.

My mom had found her Prince Charming, and someday I would find mine – and he would be just like my dad!

THE WELL

The well on the farm was very scary to me. It was underground and held all the water we used to wash and cook with. The grown-ups told me that if I fell into the well they could not help me because it was one hundred feet deep. Since I was only about a couple of feet tall, that seemed very, very deep to me. It had a very heavy, thick cement slab on top, but I stayed away just in case!

One very hot summer there was no more water in the well, so Grandpa called the fire station, and the firemen came and took off the cement slab and poured water into the well with their fire hoses. It was so exciting and I got to put on the helmet of one of the firemen, but it was too big.

VACATION

Family vacations, airplanes, faraway places, toys, sand castles and real castles are what vacations are all about. The airline asked us if they could take our picture for advertising purposes because we were the largest family they had ever had flying together – that was so cool!

ANIMAL LIFE

How much love does a mama goat have for her Billy goat baby? Who's to say it's less than a new human mother's love for her child? It is just that they show it differently. If you spent some time with them, you would understand.

FAVORITE PLACE

My favorite place was the farm. It allowed me to embrace nature and all its wonderful creations; the many different farm animals, the beauty of the land, how living creatures interact and the peacefulness of it all.

CHICKEN COOP

No, (you probably already guessed) I was not a perfect child – but I did have such fun! Whenever I wandered into the chicken coop, mischief was on my mind. I got such a kick out of scaring the chickens! I would scream and the chickens would crash into one another, feathers flying. It was the highlight of my childhood days. I never figured out how my Grandpa knew I was in the chicken coop. I was very careful to make sure no one was around when I went in there. It wasn't until I was much older that I figured out that the reason Grandpa had chickens was so he could sell the eggs at market. When I scared the chickens, they would not lay eggs that day. And anyway, he could see all the feathers floating around!

KIRBY RATS

The "Kirby Rats" were our next-door neighbors. How they came by that name is hard to say; probably it was the result of some stupid disagreement between the two families way back when. So they became the "Kirby Rats" forevermore!

It seems that everyone has a bad neighbor, doesn't it? They are either next door or down the street. If your home is your castle, then this is truly an inconvenience. Either they know it all, keep junk piled high next to your yard, have a dog that never stops barking, are very noisy or very rude. Not much you can do about it; just try to ignore them if you can!

HAY AND COWS

The color of gold, tall and high and as far as I could see. The cows' favorite food and grandpa's biggest pain! "Don't go near the cows," Grandpa would always warn me. "They're mean!" Well, I thought, maybe they thought someone wanted to steal their hay. It looked so soft to the touch, but it was actually scratchy and stiff when you lay on it. Why did the farmers roll it into a big ball? Was this some kind of contest for adults? I asked my grandpa this question, but he just laughed.

BROCCOLI

I don't know why I ever thought that broccoli could fit up my nose. It was a stupid idea, but then a five-year-old probably doesn't have many smart ideas. Lying in the vegetable garden, I guess I was bored. That is the only reason I can think of now! Anyway, it would never happen again. The hospital was not a pleasant place and I was really scared. They didn't have to tell me twice!

HORSES

Horses are the most beautiful creatures on earth. When I was little I got to ride on a big horse that lived on the farm, but then I got scared because it was so tall. So I decided to just feed him carrots and watch him run.

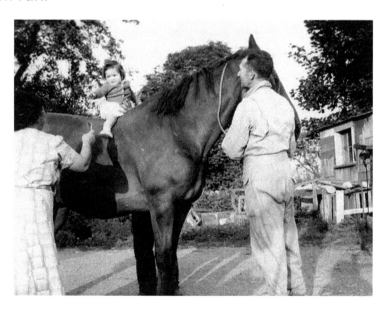

SCHOOL

School at first was very difficult for me, and riding the school bus was the worst! There I was completely alone surrounded by a bus load of happy children all talking and laughing at once and I couldn't join in. I couldn't join in because on the farm my family only spoke Portuguese and I didn't know what the children were saying. I didn't know English.

In time, with the help of my wonderful teacher, I learned how to speak in English, made friends, and began to enjoy the daily school bus rides to and from school.

In school, I couldn't stand the A's: algebra, arithmetic, anxiety, allergies.
The B's were better: boys, bras, beauty products, bathroom breaks.
But the C's were the best: concerts, chocolate, candy!

GRANDMA SLEEPING

Grandma was lying down, asleep in a strange house. Why was she so cold? Why was everyone crying? I had to get out of that strange place. I felt like I was being choked. Outside, Mom tried to explain as we piled into the hearse. Worst day of my young life!

"Deep peace of the quiet earth to you. Deep peace to you."
—from a Gaelic blessing

My grandmother was in heaven with the angels now. I hoped she was happy. I missed her very much! My cat, Saki, was also an angel; the only difference was that she was an angel cat. I was sure they all hung out together, though.

THE SADDEST PLACE OF ALL

There is a place high on a hill, the ocean far below. The green of the grass is interrupted only by cement slabs here and there. The trees have seen it all and bend over in tears... the histories of loved ones who travel this road not willingly. The road winds to and fro, only to stop here. Do not pass GO, do not collect $200. The game is over.

> **"Death is that state in which one exists only in the memory of others – which is why it is not the end."**
> **—Unknown**

FATIMA

When I was ten years old, we went to Europe on vacation, and one of the places we went to was Fatima. I experienced a miracle there, and that is why I now believe.

It was a beautiful day; the sun was shining. There was a long courtyard that stretched from where we parked the car to the church. As we were walking across it towards the church, it started to pour, and we got wet. I mean really soaked because we had no umbrellas! Suddenly the clouds went away and the sun came back out, and I realized we were all completely dry! No one could explain it. The experience left a lasting impression on me. I'm so glad we went there.

"The best and most beautiful things in the world cannot be seen or even touched. They must be felt with the heart."

—Helen Keller

CHAPTER 2

TEENAGE DREAMS

TRANSPORTATION

As a teenager, transportation was a very important part of my life; it allowed me to see my friends and go places. Dad's VW Bug for the night, a bus to the mall, or Mom and Dad as chauffeurs were all part of the everyday schedule.

LEARNING TO DRIVE

When I turned sixteen, the first thing I wanted was to get my driver's license. The problem was that all of Dad's cars had manual transmissions, so he said I needed to learn how to drive with a manual before I could go and apply for my license.

Dad found a quiet side street in town that went straight up a large hill, with a stop sign at the top. He said, "When you can balance the car at the top of the hill so it does not roll backwards, you can apply for your driver's license." I thought, how hard can that be?

After about two months of "going up the mountain" every Saturday morning and coming home in tears, I finally did it! Today I can thank my father that I can drive any vehicle, regardless of the type of transmission. It comes in handy!

> **"Oh, Lord, won't you buy me a Mercedes Benz? My friends all drive Porsches, I must make amends."**
> **—Janis Joplin**

I NEVER MET A CAR I COULDN'T NAME

They say, "If you love something, let it go." But I say, "If you love something, give it a name."

All of my favorite cars have names. My very first car (a Ford Falcon) was shiny black with a red leather interior and three on the wheel. It was a gorgeous gem, but it was a hand-me-down from my brother, who had had an accident with it. I received it with the passenger door damaged beyond repair. Being a great dad, my dad got a new door for the car, but the door was white, so my baby was christened "the Skunk."

Much later on, my tastes went to the exotic. A dark blue Triumph Spitfire landed in my lap. You got it;

another hand-me-down from my brother. Its name was "Midnight" and on weekends we hit the local dance places in it.

I still couldn't get enough of the exotic and didn't want any more hand-me-downs, so I purchased a 944 – as in Porsche. I named it "JJ," as my tastes in men were starting to develop.

I asked around and found that most people didn't name their cars like I did. Perhaps they didn't come from a car-crazy family like mine, or maybe they just weren't very creative; I don't know! But I do know they were missing out on a lot of fun – especially with the top down!

WOMEN & CAR REPAIRS

I will share some tips regarding car repairs from a woman who got taken:

1. Always ask for the old parts back, even if you are going to throw them away! Maybe they won't rip you off if they think you have a clue about the work you are asking them to do on your car.

2. Keep all of your receipts. You may never use them again, but it sure looks good when you go to sell the car!

3. Better still; if you can afford it, always buy a new car every few years, so you won't have a lot of repairs to pay for!

SINGER SEWING CENTER

During my early teenage years, Mom decided I needed to learn how to sew. She had inherited Grandma's sewing machine. Grandma had sewed and hemmed Mom's clothes, as she had done for my dolls, but Mom had never learned how to sew. So Mom decided that I had to learn because it was too expensive to go to a seamstress all the time.

My summers were for going to the park, swimming and playing table pool with all my friends. I did not want to spend my time learning how to sew! But Mom won the argument and that summer I started taking sewing lessons at the Singer Sewing Center. Once a week, every Saturday, I went there for hours to learn the basics of sewing. To my surprise, I found that I actually enjoyed it!

Our final sewing project in class that summer was to pick out a pattern, purchase the material, and create an outfit for ourselves that would be judged by a panel of sewing experts from Singer. We were told that about two hundred girls had entered the state competition.

The competition consisted of three age groups: Tween, Teenage, and Young Adult. A winner would be chosen from each. Our teacher would be in class only for guidance as we created our outfits. Each state had its own competition that summer and the winners from all of the states would then go on to the National Singer Sewing Competition.

I was so excited as I created a two-piece skirt suit with a matching scarf to be judged in the competition. I spent many hours working on all the details to achieve perfection. I really wanted my suit to win. And my hard work paid off! I won the Annual Singer Sewing Contest for my age group, Tween, in Connecticut. I was surprised that I won, but what a sense of accomplishment I got from it!

My picture was taken and put into the local newspaper that weekend. Of course, Mom cut out the article and showed it to all her friends. I also received a framed plaque with my name on it, which I hung up in my room at home.

My suit went on to the national competition, but it didn't make the final cut. That was okay, because I got great satisfaction from it anyway. However, now I had to sew anything Mom needed. So I guess we both won!

PRINCESS DOLLY

As you know, when we lived on my grandparents' farm, my family had many dogs. As a teenager, I was able to pick out my own dog, and I named her "Princess Dolly." I wish you could have seen her. There was always love in her eyes – a love that was just for me. She was something special to me. When I was feeling down, she was sad too. When I was sick, she played nurse in her own little way. To me, she was one of the most beautiful of her kind, my little German Shepherd dog.

FAVORITE PLACE

Living on the farm as a child, I developed a strong appreciation for the outdoors. That's probably why I loved camping out at Burlingame. Like most teen-agers, I loved going to the beach. A few of us girls got the idea to stay at a campsite for a week or two, since school was out for summer. Camping was so much fun – getting a tan at the beach by day, and then coming back to camp, taking a shower and cooking hot dogs over the fire... the best!

MY FAVORITE HOLIDAY

It had to be Halloween because it was so much fun to dress up as crazy as we wanted! Although I loved summer, October had to be my favorite month of the year because Halloween is in October. I loved getting dressed up in costume and going to Halloween parties.

VACATION

Every teenager lives for vacation, and I was no exception. My family and I loved Disney. I also loved the game room, swimming in the pool, waterslides, cool tee-shirts, and let's not forget checking out the boys at the hotel – now that's a great vacation!

DAD'S HOBBY

My dad had a special hobby. He was a ham radio operator in his spare time. He had a "radio shack" downstairs, where he communicated with new friends from all over the world with his ham radios.

He once phone-patched through a call from Peru to New York for a doctor who was trying to reach a clinic in New York to inquire about a new drug that might save the life of one of his patients, a little girl who was dying. Later, Dad received thanks because the doctor was able to locate the drug, which was shipped to the dying girl. However, Dad never did learn whether it saved her life.

Morse Code was one of the requirements of the FCC Amateur Radio Operators License Exam, which my dad had successfully passed years ago, and he was very proficient in Morse Code. Because of this, he was asked to join the Boy Scouts as a Morse Code Scout Leader. The Boy Scouts would learn from Dad how to improve their receiving and transmitting speed and accuracy in Morse Code to achieve a Radio Merit Badge. I know my dad enjoyed the opportunity, and many of his Scouts went on to win their Radio Merit Badge because of him.

Today, the Boy Scouts Radio Merit Badge has been renamed the Signs, Signals and Codes Merit Badge, but Morse Code is still listed as a skill in the Boy Scout Handbook.

GRADUATION

Ever since my grandmother died, I have been fas-
cinated with medicine and how it could help people
like my grandmother live longer. I also decided that
I wanted to be a doctor. I often watched the Medical
Channel on TV and was completely in awe when
watching knee operations and how they were per-
formed, the preparations and precautions taken to
prevent infection, the tools used and the procedures
followed. It was fascinating to me! Any medical or
hospital-related TV show was my choice to watch.
Mom and Dad thought this was a bit strange, but I
didn't care. They'd much rather watch CNN and other news channels instead.

I didn't even tell them that I had already picked out
my specialty. I wanted to be an orthopedic surgeon.
So when it came time to apply to various colleges,
I knew that I would be choosing schools that could
lead me to a medical career path. Unfortunately, my
dream was not realized, for when I told Mom and
Dad, they said, "We can't afford medical school for
you. You will need to pick another career choice." I
was devastated but Mom had been a teacher, so I
chose teaching because I didn't know what else to
pick. Not my first choice, but I guess it was okay. So I
got my Bachelor of Science Degree in Education and
then started looking for a teaching job, preferably in
the same town, or at least close by.

When I got my degree, there weren't many local teaching jobs available. Apparently everyone who went into teaching in my area stayed until retirement – my luck! I even took a one-year job as a teacher's aide, figuring that I'd be the first to know who was retiring and have dibs, but that didn't work out either.

So I applied for a Training Department job at a local insurance company, which, surprisingly, I found I really liked.

SMART WOMEN

Early on, I learned that men don't usually like smart women. They like women who just look good. So, I thought, impress them with looks and keep the smart side to yourself for a while!

SHELLS

There is something special about shells to me and as a teenager, I started to collect them. Little perfect treasures! They came in all shapes and lots of colors. The large ones were hard to find. A day at the beach could bring many on shore, especially after a storm.

I collect shells as many people do; in jars and standing alone, they fit into any décor! They last forever and they speak to you, bringing peace and tranquility.

Shells are used in crafts, jewelry, and displayed in museums, as well. It is so interesting that shells are millions of years old and there are different varieties throughout the world. No matter how many you collect, there always seems to be more!

BOOKS

I have always loved books. My bookcase at home can attest to that! Mom was always complaining that I was ignoring my chores, but I loved to read and had trouble putting down a book midway. Guess you could call me a bookworm!

That's why I can't write a book without talking about wonderful books! The in-your-hands kind of book: hard-cover, soft-cover, paperbacks too – their smell, their touch, their allure.

And the eReaders: Kindles, Nooks, tablets too; their ease and portability, read forever, everywhere – in schools, on buses, in the library, at the beach, and even in your own backyard.

New releases, coming soon, old favorites, new writers, bestsellers, bargain books and attic finds – summer reading, winter reading, love of reading, love a good book!

Let's not forget cookbooks, history and mystery, art and religion, diet and fitness, romance and science fiction, sports, fiction and non-fiction – too many to choose from!

COOKBOOKS

Early in life, I learned the importance of books when I received a cookbook series (A through Z) containing colorful pictures of all the finished recipes. Moral of the story: if you cook, they may or may not come. But if you cook WELL, they will come!

CHAPTER **3**

TWENTYSOMETHING

LIVING AT HOME

Living at my parents' house was great. Mom did all the cooking and cleaning. She would wake me up every morning to go to work. When I came home from work, dinner would always be ready. I was living a life of leisure.

SLEEPING IN

No matter how much I practice, one thing I guess I'll never be any better at is getting up in the morning!

ORPHAN ANNIE

My twenties were a time of endless search to find myself. It was a time of great ideas, but some of them produced not-so-great results. Like the time I decided to dye my hair red. Not bad at all, I thought. Then I decided to go and get a body wave. I guess I didn't realize what I looked like until one Saturday morning when I was clothes shopping at Westfarms Mall. As I was looking around and trying to decide what store to go into first, someone called out to me, "You're going in the wrong direction. The contest is down the hall." "What contest?" I asked. "The Orphan Annie contest. Isn't that what you're here for?"

So embarrassing!

However, I decided to make the most of it and posed for a picture with my dog, Lord Cinnamon, a Lhasa Apso, to record the event for posterity!

THE "FALL"

After the body wave relaxed a bit, I changed my hair color to dark brown and then got my hair straightened. Wigs were very popular then, so I purchased a "fall," which would make me look like I had really long hair.

It clipped onto the top of my hair and cascaded down my back – very sexy, I thought. All I had to do was take a small section of hair and comb it over the fall to hide the clip. I attached a fancy barrette and I was now a long-haired beauty, or so I thought!

I decided to wear the fall on a blind date. Unfortunately for me, my date decided to try to kiss me while running his hands through my hair. You guessed it – the fall started to fall off! Guess I scared him away. Too bad; he seemed like such a nice guy, too.

MOTORCYCLES

Then there was the time I decided I would try to drive my brother's motorcycle around the block. I guess I was a bit of a tomboy. I had no problem driving the motorcycle, and I was really enjoying myself. But then I wanted to stop and didn't know how, so I started screaming for my brother to come out of the house and help me. I think the neighbors thought I was crazy as I went round and round the block, screaming for my brother. It seemed like I waited for him forever. When my brother finally did come out of the house, he helped me stop the motorcycle and turn off the ignition. However, he was not too happy with me and said I could never drive his motorcycle again.

MY FAVORITE HOLIDAY

Every day I was off from work! No, really – my favorite holiday still is and always will be Halloween.

FAVORITE PLACE

By the ocean in Rhode Island! The smells, the waves, the birds, the rocks, the shells, the sand, the peacefulness!

One thing I really enjoyed, and could spend an entire day doing, was collecting sea glass from the rocks at Easton's Beach in Newport. So much fun, and a great way to get a tan too!

VALERIE'S WEDDING

"It is the most beautiful dress I've ever seen," I said as I twirled in the mirror. "And it's so elegant!" The marabou sleeves were so "on the runway," and the dress was one of my favorite colors to boot. "I'll take it!" I said. "Well, don't you look like a little princess in pink, like right out of a fairy tale," the saleswoman said.

Every time I found a dressy dress that I liked, I would always have to shorten it or tailor it somehow because I was short. Not this one, though, and that's how I knew it was meant for me!

Mom was born in Newport, Rhode Island and had been best friends with a woman named Mary for some forty years. After we moved to Connecticut, Mom and Mary talked on the phone constantly. One day we learned that Mary's beautiful only daughter, Valerie (who was also my friend), was getting married. Mary was planning an all-out fabulous wedding for her daughter and we were invited.

It was going to be a military-style wedding, to be held at the Newport Naval Base, where Valerie's fiancé was stationed.

We were all so looking forward to the Saturday-morning wedding. Dad had to work that Friday night, so on Saturday morning very early, we packed our bags into the car's truck because we were going to stay the entire weekend in Newport.

Mary had rented an RV for us at to stay in after the wedding, at a campground nearby in Middletown, Rhode Island. All of her out-of-state relatives were coming to the wedding and would be staying at her house, so there was no room for us to stay there.

So the three of us piled into the car for the two-hour drive to the wedding. Mom and Dad sat in the front seats and I sat in the back seat. I was so excited, but I started to feel a bit uncomfortable during the long drive, as I was all dressed up and couldn't move out of fear that my dress would become wrinkled. When we finally arrived at the Naval Base, Mary ran out to greet us, saying she was so happy we were able to come!

The weather had cooperated; it was a beautiful sunny day. The wedding party had their pictures taken by the water outside and then formed an archway for the newly married couple to walk under as they entered the ballroom for the wedding reception. What a sight!

Valerie looked the prettiest I had ever seen her, all dressed up in a gorgeous white wedding gown studded with pearls. Her husband looked so very proud. This is what life was all about. Someday, I dreamed, I would have a wedding like this, too.

WEDDING RECEPTION

The ballroom for the wedding reception was gorgeously decorated: fountains flowing with champagne, chandeliers everywhere on the ceiling, beautiful white tablecloths and decorations on the tables, and twinkling lights around every pole. Then the band started to play.

Mom and Dad were drinking Vino Verde, a Portuguese white wine. As they laughed and talked with Valerie's parents, it seemed like the four of them were reliving old times, back when they were young and just getting married themselves. Mom didn't usually drink and I had never seen her drink this much. She was laughing and giggling. Dad had his arm around her and they seemed so happy together. Someday, I thought, I would get married and have children of my own. I hoped for a husband who would hold my hand like Dad did with Mom all the time.

I think my family might have been one of the last ones to leave the wedding reception. What a great wedding! I was so happy for Valerie.

RV #12

As we got into the car, Dad said he had the key to RV #12, which was in the campground a couple of miles away, and that was where we were going to sleep that night. He told us we had to be very quiet because it was almost 2:00 a.m. and everyone at the campground was probably sleeping at that hour.

A short time later, we pulled into the RV campground. No one was around at this late hour. We looked for RV #12 and discovered the oddest thing: the numbers were between the RVs, not in front of them. Ours could have been the one on the left or the one on the right of the #12 sign. We didn't see any cars parked near either one.

As we got out of the car and gathered up our bags, Mom giggled and chattered about how much fun she had had tonight and that she hadn't stayed up this late in years; then she tripped getting out of the car. That was when I realized she was drunk. Wow, Mom drunk! Now that was a first!

Dad said, "I think ours is the one on the left," so we gathered up our suitcases and climbed the stairs to the RV. "The door is open," Dad said, so we knew we had picked the right one.

As we settled in, I decided to make coffee for all of us so we could sit down and rehash the wonderful day we'd had. We were all talking, laughing and enjoying ourselves, and Dad turned on the TV. As I was making coffee, he went to check out the sleeping quarters in the back of the RV. Suddenly he ran back into the kitchen and announced that there was someone sleeping in the back bedroom! We thought he was joking and Mom and I started laughing hysterically. "I'm not kidding!" he said, which made us laugh even harder. Then we realized it was true and we all rushed at once to get out of the RV, grabbing our bags and tripping over each other. I shut off the stove and snatched up my shoes. We almost fell down the stairs. What a sight we were; drunk and with tears in our eyes from laughing so much.

"Well, I guess it must be the RV to the right!" Dad said, which started us laughing hysterically again.

"This RV is locked, so keep your fingers crossed that the key fits!" It did, and we all settled into #12 RV on the right, falling asleep almost immediately (without any further unexpected tenants).

The next morning, groggy and hung over, we asked ourselves if that had really happened last night! We realized that they could have had a gun or called the police. We could have been killed! Wow, we were really lucky.

We never did see anyone leave the RV on the left as we drove away. It was the most embarrassing thing that ever happened to me, but sharing that experience brought Mom, Dad, and me so much closer. I saw them in a different light; that weekend we were friends, not parents and daughter. The child inside all of us came out to play for those two days and it was special! How I wanted a relationship someday like Mom and Dad had. It was so obvious they were still so much in love.

TENNIS

I started taking tennis lessons in my twenties and spent a lot of time on the court. I even joined the Glenbrooke Swim and Tennis Club so I could practice on their Har-Tru clay courts. I played tennis almost every day, and even went on a week-long trip to a tennis camp in Killington, Vermont, to perfect my skills.

But the really special times were going to the US Tennis Open in New York every year, watching my favorites play (like Sabatini and Agassi) and dreaming of playing like that myself someday! I enjoyed playing tennis so much that I wrote a poem about it.

"ODE TO A TENNIS PLAYER"

May your backhand remain strong and the touch of your drop shot light.

May your tournament wins grow as the errors decrease.

May your grip stay firm, your feet dance sweetly, and your focus remain strong.

This is what I wish for you, my favorite tennis partner!

DAVIS CUP QUARTER FINAL CHAMPIONSHIP IN NEWPORT

I was so excited I was able to get tickets to the Davis Cup Quarter Finals in Newport, Rhode Island that year. John McEnroe and Coach Brad Gilbert would lead the USA team, while Emilio and Javier Sanchez would defend Spain. It was so very exciting to watch! I even got some of the players' autographs on my program book.

SHOES

Besides tennis, my favorite thing to do was buy shoes. I loved shoes! Some say it is an addiction, while others say it is a necessary evil. Shoes can hurt, even when they look fabulous. They make us taller (I liked that) and they come in many shapes and sizes. Unfortunately, once addicted to shoes, there is no turning back.

So the excuses flowed: new season, old boots, new colors, vacation, special occasion, sale... I loved my new shoes – now I needed an outfit to match!

Whatever the pull, the inability to resist was very powerful. And the styles: high heels, low heels, kitten heels, flats, sandals, wedges, gladiators, slides, flip-flops/thongs, running shoes, tennis shoes, walking shoes, evening shoes – how could you help but not have a few of each? I needed a bigger closet!

FUR BABIES

For me, life is not complete without my fur babies. I have always had at least two pets since I was a child. Maybe growing up on a farm is why – maybe not – but either way, sharing life with fur babies, big or small, is special, and not always predictable. Cats who eat shoes, sit on top of refrigerators, or love to play in water might not be the norm, but definitely possible. I've seen it.

There are dogs who are needy, shaking violently and red-eyed as they are led into doggie day camp. There are large dogs who only want to play with little dogs but are afraid of dogs their own size. I've seen it all!

But all of them, dogs and cats, are very lovable. The childlike attention they crave, their antics, the softness of their fur and playfulness only increases the warm closeness you feel for them.

READY, SET, ACTION

I keep a pen and paper handy on my nightstand. You never know when it might come in handy because most of us are great inventors, movie directors, or exciting sports figures, champions at any sport, right? The only problem is that we do our best work in the middle of the night! A great idea you have while sleeping becomes fuzzy when the alarm clock goes off.

CHAPTER 4

REAL LIFE

BEST DAY OF MY LIFE!

I was invited to another friend's wedding and I was very excited to go. Little did I know it would be a day I would never forget. At the reception, after the beautiful wedding ceremony and a delicious meal, the band started to play. Suddenly a gorgeous man, older than I was, a real Robert Redford type, asked me to dance. His name was Ralph and he was tall, blond, blue-eyed, and had a beautiful smile. I think my heart actually skipped a beat for a moment.

As we danced, I found out that Ralph was a Marine, just home from the Service and was living with his mother, who had been divorced from his dad for years. His dad had moved out West to California. I was pleased to find a guy who seemed so responsible and caring. His mother, on the other hand, was not too happy with me when I met her. I think she thought I was taking her son away from her.

BEST YEAR OF MY LIFE!

The next year was one of the happiest years of my life, especially the day Ralph asked me to marry him. My parents had grown to love him and were so pleased with our news, as was Ralph's beautiful sister, who I immediately got along with very well.

Ralph's mother, on the other hand, actually told me that I was trying to take him away from her. What could I say? This was starting to get difficult!

WEDDING PLANS

As we started to plan our wedding, Ralph's mother said she would not attend her son's wedding if he invited his dad, or if he even contacted him to let him know he was getting married. She was afraid his dad would show up. She was still very bitter about their divorce even after all these years.

To please his mother, we never invited his dad to our wedding. We both felt terrible about this, but Ralph had been living with his mom so he felt it was the right thing to do at the time. I do know this upset him very much, but he wanted to please his mom.

WEDDING DAY

My parents wanted me to have a fabulous wedding day and they paid for everything. Our job was to plan (and pay for) a fabulous honeymoon to match, they said with a smile.

So my beautiful wedding to Ralph took place at the country club on a gorgeous fall day, with music, flowers everywhere, and lots of pictures taken. We had about 300 guests in attendance and everyone had a great time. It was a fairytale wedding, and I felt like a princess. We would be happy ever after; I was so sure of it!

HONEYMOON

Our honeymoon was in paradise. Yes, paradise has a name – Hawaii! It is all they say it is: the most beautiful tropical island with lots of palm trees and beautiful beaches. My favorite place was by the ocean. The smells, the waves, the birds, the rocks, the shells, the sand, the peacefulness! The palm trees were everywhere, bending in rhythm to the afternoon breezes.

Although the plane ride to get to Hawaii seemed to take forever, it was all worth it when we finally arrived. As we disembarked from the plane, beautiful women in Polynesian gowns greeted us, saying "Aloha" and placing real flower leis around our necks. So exciting and different!

We spent the next ten days sitting on the beach getting a great tan, touring the island, and we even did some shopping.

One of my favorite memories of Hawaii was going to the Don Ho Show at the Polynesian Palace Theater. Don Ho was a great entertainer and headlined Waikiki's most popular show at that time. On stage along with many Hulu dancers, Don Ho sang many songs, including his best-selling "Tiny Bubbles", as part of his nightclub act. Each song brought cheers from the audience.

To me, Don Ho was an extraordinary entertainer and his show was one of the highlights of our visit to Hawaii.

We also went to other awesome nightspots, dancing till dawn. Such fun! I had met and married the man of my dreams. I was so in love, and so happy. We both were.

"I think if you can dance and be free and not embarrassed, you can rule the world."
—Amy Poehler

AFTER THE HONEYMOON

We were a regular couple when we got back home with wonderful memories of our honeymoon, and we couldn't wait to settle down and start our married life together, and someday have children.

We rented a small apartment and went to work every day; me to an insurance company and Ralph in the family business. On weekends we went to the movies, camped out, and occasionally went out to dinner.

When we could afford it, we went dancing on week-end evenings. Ralph loved to dance and we simply enjoyed being with each other. Weekends always flew by too fast!

Once a month Ralph went to the VA Hospital in the next state, which he said was routine for anyone coming home from the service. "Just checking in," he said, and I thought it was very nice for them to see veterans so often.

LOVE LETTERS

We were so happy those first few years. Ralph was a true romantic and would write me love poems, most of which I have kept all these years. I am sharing three of them with you.

"Hello. I'm the ionosphere of Exultain, escape from sometimes and somewhere to always and forever. My feelings are bound inside of my body which is only superficial. My spirit is great and real for you."

"In love is where I want to be. Like the stream who has a tree to keep its waters from running over so the grass will not drown. I am here, you are there. The stream is ours; helped by the tree, to help the tree so that the grass may grow, so it may not drown. Our love is long and winding like the stream. It is sturdy like the tree. And it will grow forever like the grass."

"My only reality is the Past. To know the Present is my Goal. Looking back, I try to see ahead. And as I run only to find I have not Progressed, I keep myself together. And at this moment I wonder Why? With all the running I have done... And with my sentence to continue, I still don't know which way to go. But now I turn... I see a Road. It leads not to or fro. And for a moment I think that I would die. But something back there tells me I'll get by. So, as if suspended, I'll kick and push. And although I'll never know it, I'll be there. Or... am I there now?"

SUNDAY DINNER WITH PARENTS

Mom and Dad were always inviting us to Sunday dinner. We had a large family, and it was their attempt at keeping track of all of us. Dad gave the holiday toast with delicious port wine, and always made the salad with his special secret-recipe salad dressing. Mom served her delicious desserts.

There was always lots of food and good conversation all around, and we all helped clean up afterwards. I never realized how much I would miss Sunday dinner, and the closeness it brought to my family.

> **"Family is the most important thing in the world."**
> **—Diana, Princess of Wales**

THANKSGIVING

It was time for me to host a holiday dinner in our little apartment, so I chose Thanksgiving. What a mistake that was! The turkey was still frozen but the guests were coming in a few hours. Let's stuff it and stick it in the oven. Gosh, this was harder than I thought. Dinner guests seated, electric carving knife in hand, I, the hostess with the mostest, dug into the stuffing only to have the bag of gizzards fall out of the cavity. How embarrassing!

RALPH'S DAD

A few years went by and Ralph was increasingly talking about contacting his dad and going to visit him. He wanted his dad to meet me and see how happy we were. So we started planning and saving for a surprise visit to him out West. Of course, we couldn't tell his mom, who had never changed her attitude about Ralph's dad.

We wanted to stay for two weeks, to give Ralph enough time to bond again with his father. Because his parents had divorced when he was very young, he really didn't spend much time with his dad while growing up. It had been about five years since the last time he saw him in person.

I was very excited about going to meet him, and wanted to know more about this man, who I knew Ralph was very proud of. I found out that he had been a Minor League baseball player when he was young, a real athlete. I was very impressed and looking forward to meeting him.

VACATION OUT WEST

When we arrived in California, we rented a car and deposited our luggage at the hotel before driving to Ralph's father's house to surprise him. His dad opened the door and I couldn't believe the resemblance between him and Ralph. They looked so much alike, except that his dad had a bit of gray hair around the temples and was very thin. I now could see what Ralph would look like when he got older – still very handsome!

I met Ralph's dad's beautiful wife too, who treated us to our own large bedroom with en-suite bathroom, clean towels and linens, and a full home-cooked breakfast every morning. Both of them were so sweet and loving to us.

They refused to let us stay at the hotel and insisted that we stay with them for the entire vacation, and that we use their car whenever we wanted to go anywhere. Wow, how nice! Obviously, Ralph's dad understood the situation with his mom and didn't hold it against him. No wonder my husband was so impressed with his father! He was a really nice guy and so happy to see his son again.

DEVASTATING NEWS

Then his dad sat us down to catch up, and we got our first shock. He told us that he had lung cancer and had already had surgery to remove part of one of his lungs. Ralph was horrified, as was I. This was the man he had told me about – his athletic father, who now had trouble breathing. That was when I noticed the oxygen machine in the corner, for when he needed it on especially bad days. So sad!

Something snapped right then and there in Ralph. He became quiet and depressed for the rest of our trip. Something was seriously wrong with him and I didn't know what to do.

One evening Ralph came into the bedroom, white as a ghost. I asked him what was wrong, and he told me his dad had let him see the scar on his body from the operation. Ralph was really upset. We had planned for so long for this vacation and it was definitely not turning out as planned!

THE DEVIL OUTSIDE

Back home, everything started to unravel. Ralph said he had to go to the VA Hospital right away, but since it had only been two weeks since he had been there, I was confused. Ralph was having trouble talking to me about things, and he was barely eating or combing his hair.

It was then that Ralph told me he felt guilty for not having been in touch with his dad much sooner. He wished he had listened less to his mom, and that he had done what he thought was the right thing – inviting his dad to our wedding and staying in touch with him more often. He wished that he could have been there for his father throughout his illness, and now it might be too late.

Then one day I came home from work to find his family's company truck parked in the driveway and Ralph in bed under the covers. I asked him if he was sick, and he said, "No." Why was the company truck in the yard? He replied that he didn't remember driving it home. Where was his car? Ralph didn't remember that either. Oh my God, what was going on?

He started wearing a navy wool cap on his head in the apartment all the time. It was probably part of his uniform from his service days. It was pulled low, covering one ear all the time. I asked him why he had it on like that and he said, "It blocks out the voices." The voices? What the heck! This was turning into a nightmare…

Ralph wasn't communicating with me and seemed so detached, alone in his own world, of which I was not a part. He was afraid to go outside, saying that the devil was waiting for him out there. It looked like our dancing days were over.

One weekend morning I was making our bed when I found a large kitchen knife under his pillow. Frightened, I asked him why it was there. He said, "In case the devil decides to come inside." Oh, my God! I felt like I was in my own horror movie. This couldn't be happening! I was getting really scared.

JIMMY OLSEN

Sometimes I would find him talking to the walls and laughing. I was afraid to ask. He'd say, "Don't you hear it? It's Jimmy Olsen – you know, Superman's friend. He is so funny." I was now truly terrified of being around my own husband. And at the same time, it was heartbreaking to see him like this.

What had happened to my beautiful, strong husband – and who was this stranger? I didn't know what to do, or what to expect from day to day. When he no longer wanted to go to work, they fired him. How was I going to pay the rent, with just me working? How were we going to live? I was so upset. This situation had been going on too long and it was getting worse. I had to do something. I was having trouble functioning, not knowing what to expect next. My fairy tale was vanishing and I didn't know how to save it. I was afraid that no one would believe me but it was time to tell my parents that something was terribly wrong. Maybe they would know what to do.

A REVELATION

Mom and Dad said that we all should go to the VA Hospital with Ralph. "We need to find out what the hell is going on," Dad said. "Maybe they can tell us what is going on and help him. Neither of you can go on like this." Ralph went with us voluntarily and said goodbye to me, as if I would never see his again, as the doctor led him off. It was so freaky!

Mom, Dad, and I were called into another doctor's office, where I learned for the very first time that my husband had been diagnosed in the service with paranoid schizophrenia. He had gotten treatment then, which appeared to cure him. That's why he went to the VA hospital every month, to get more medicine. Wow, was I stupid or what! Love really is blind.

I was asked if we had any children and told in no uncertain terms to never let that happen if he got out of the hospital. I was told that these brain-altering diseases were, in some cases, hereditary, so I must never take the chance! I was very upset hearing this, as we had planned to start a family soon. I was beginning to understand the magnitude of our problems.

The doctor wanted to know what had happened that brought us there that day, so I told him of the past few years, the visit to Ralph's dad, how his dad was so sick, and Ralph's reaction to it. The doctor said that episodes of extreme stress can trigger the psychosis. That must have been what happened to Ralph when he learned his father was so very sick and possibly dying.

The drive home was very quiet; Dad, Mom, and I were still in a state of shock and disbelief. My head was spinning. There was no prediction of how long Ralph would have to stay in the hospital, or if he would ever be well enough to leave. I felt like I was drowning and to top it off, his mother blamed me for what was happening to her son! Oh, my God! What was I going to do? What was happening to our marriage? I had never been so upset in my entire life and I was not prepared mentally to handle any of this.

AFTERMATH

After that day, I couldn't function, so I decided it would be best for me to move back in with Mom and Dad. I couldn't even concentrate enough to go to work; I didn't even want to get out of bed. All I did was cry and cry. My heart was broken.

I am not sure how long I was in that state of mind. My parents were pushing for me to see a psychiatrist. After much deliberation, I reluctantly filed for divorce. I couldn't handle the pressure anymore. I wanted out of this nightmare! My parents felt that divorce was a bad decision, but what was I going to do? I felt so depressed. I know my parents were embarrassed because there had never been a divorce before in my family. I felt like such a loser.

GRAPES & VINYL

There is a correlation between love and marriage, skinny and fat. We all know that *divorce* equals *fat*. So if that's where you are at, first invest in some Kleenex stock, purchase a gallon of wine, and get out those old DVDs!

HEALING TIME

Time does heal all wounds, it's really true... even deep, unthinkable wounds like mine. Ralph was in the hospital for over a year that I know of. We wrote to each other occasionally and I cried as I read each of his letters. Then one day he stopped writing to me and I couldn't bring myself to go to the VA Hospital to find out where he was. I was still hurting so much.

A few years later I found out that Ralph had died. A friend told me that his obituary was in the paper.

Sadness, emptiness, anger, and hurt surfaced in me again, all at once. He was gone. Nothing would ever be the same. It was so hard to imagine death at such an early age.

I decided to go to his wake even though I was nervous about seeing his mother, but she wasn't there. Apparently she had developed Alzheimer's a couple of years before and was in a nursing home. She didn't even know her son had died. How ironic!

I wanted to go and say goodbye to the man I had always loved – even now. His beautiful sister and her children were all there, surprised but happy to see me. She hugged me close and we both cried for a wonderful man who had been given a terrible disease to suffer, this heavy burden to bear. She asked me to join in with her to greet the guests attending the wake. She said I was still her sister-in-law and a big part of Ralph's life. I was so thankful for their kindness. All in all, it was a tough day, but going to Ralph's wake did help me heal. I couldn't bring myself to go to the funeral, though; the wake was more than I could handle.

With time, I have learned to cherish the good memories of our married life together, and there were many before Ralph got sick. I did my best to put all the sadness behind me, for the most part, and move on.

CHAPTER 5

CAREER

GETTING LAID OFF

Eventually I went back to working in the Training Department at the insurance company. I stayed there for a number of years, until I got laid off.

As Ronald Reagan once put it: "Recession is when your neighbor gets laid off. Depression is when you get laid off." It is so true!

How does one get a crystal paperweight for excellence in customer service and three months later, a pink slip? It does not compute! But that is our world today, like it or not. Look forward, not back, is the best advice one can give or get.

THE PERFECT JOB

Being laid off, I had plenty of time to look for another job. The perfect job appeared one day that included my two favorite professions: healthcare and teaching. It was at another local insurance company. I applied and got the job!

It was a great opportunity. I would be a Nationwide Training Liaison to medical personnel in Family Care Centers around the country who were partnering with the insurance company to deliver quality patient care. The company had instructors in numerous parts of the country, with the home office in Connecticut. I was to be stationed in Connecticut, but train and travel as needed around the country.

My role was to participate in the development of customized training materials for each state, to facilitate client classes on-site, and then to provide support during the initial rollout of each client's new EPIC Medical Practice Management computer system. I was to assist their physicians and medical office staff with live practice use of the new system, so they would become proficient.

But first I had to learn the medical billing functions of the computer system, the front office data entry processes, and patient registration steps to be able to perform my job successfully. This position included a lot of nationwide travel, but it sounded exciting and it was just what I needed at the moment.

CLEVELAND, OHIO

The Cleveland Training Center was where I was to learn all of the system's functions the various medical personnel would need to learn, including how to create customized patient reports as needed, and the role of the system in all their medical processes. The training curriculum I had to master was six weeks long and included classroom training, hands-on practice, shadowing of instructors, and teach-backs, where we had to present the material we just learned to those who were already proficient with the system, in preparation for teaching the clients and answering any questions they might have. I have to say there was a point in the middle of all this that I was about to give up and go home – it was not easy and I missed my parents – but I wasn't going to be defeated! So I stayed. As Amelia Earhart said, "You can do anything you decide to do."

I kept trying to get tickets to see the Cleveland Indians, but they were always sold out on weekends. I did, however, get to visit a lot of the tourist attractions around Cleveland. One unusual experience was walking ankle-deep in water in "The Flats," an area near the lake, when it rained. One minute it was starting to rain, and the next there was a flood! I was suddenly soaked, my shoes squishing as I walked on the sidewalk. I had never seen anything like this anywhere else! They called it "The Lake Effect," referring to Lake Erie.

Well, I survived my six weeks in Cleveland, and went home to do paperwork in the office, wash clothes, and take a breather until my first teaching assignment. With an organization across the country of twenty-plus HealthWays Medical Centers, and still growing, I was anticipating getting to travel to many different locations. This was a new approach to the practice of family medicine, and I was very excited to be a part of this growing initiative. Their model was to put patient care first! Each center was staffed with a medical director, primary care physicians, pediatricians, internal medicine physicians, nurses and nurse practitioners, technicians, and patient service representatives, who manned the front desk. The staff routinely saw patients for a variety of illnesses, providing health assessments and immunizations, emergency care, and referrals for hospital admittances. They also provided exceptional customer service to their patients during flu season. I would say, on average, each medical center served approximately 500–1,000 patients a month.

CHICAGO, ILLINOIS

My first real training assignment was in Chicago – in December! I simply could not believe the extreme cold and wind I encountered there. I'll give you an example. One night after work, a couple of colleagues and I decided to go out to a well-known steakhouse for dinner in downtown Chicago. Because of its popularity, even though we had reservations, there was no parking for a block around the restaurant! We had to park a block away in a commercial parking lot and walk to the restaurant. By the time we got to the restaurant, my eyelashes were caked in ice and my hair was all swept around my face.

CHERYL

It was in Chicago that I met a new friend. Cheryl was also a trainer like me, but she lived in a suburb of Chicago. We quickly became friends. Every month our company held team meetings in the Connecticut home office, so Cheryl had to travel a lot to Connecticut, as I did to Chicago. When we were training in separate locations, we always kept in touch via phone or email. Cheryl and I became good friends and still are to this day.

THE RACQUETBALL COURT

Chicago had four HealthWays Medical Centers at that time, and Wheaton Clinic (a huge multistory hospital in Wheaton, Illinois) was where I was stationed to teach classes. This seemed routine, but I didn't expect to be teaching those classes in the clinic's basement, a former racquetball court used by staff physicians years ago when they were on a break. Yes, I said a former racquetball court. Can you imagine? Cheryl and I co-taught that week together. The acoustics in the room were terrible, but the students were great. Still, it was quite a challenge!

MICHIGAN AVENUE

Because the winter weather was so extreme when I was working in Chicago, I was not surprised, one weekend while Cheryl and I were shopping, to see that most of the women at the large mall on Michigan Avenue were wearing real fur coats. They were really needed in this climate!

SIGHTSEEING IN CHICAGO

I felt very fortunate that Cheryl showed me all around Chicago when we weren't working, so I was able to see what the city had to offer two single women.

We even visited the Sears Tower and took the elevator to the very top of the 110 floors – the Skydeck – to get a fabulous view of the city. But my favorite spot in all of Chicago was North Lake Shore Drive – beautiful!

EPIC – MADISON, WISCONSIN

I had the wonderful opportunity to visit the beautiful campus of the EPIC Systems Corporation in Madison, Wisconsin, whose healthcare software and patient electronic records systems we were implementing in all the HealthWays Centers throughout the country. EPIC's clinical and financial programs served multitudes of patients, doctors, and hospitals with their innovative healthcare delivery software, so I was thrilled to be invited to visit their campus and see firsthand the technology being developed.

The guided tour of EPIC's original worldwide headquarters in Wisconsin was fascinating, and the staff was very informative. This visit served to be very helpful to me when teaching at the HealthWays Centers.

CHARLOTTE, NORTH CAROLINA

My next training assignment was in Charlotte, North Carolina. At that time, there were only three Charlotte HealthWays Centers in the city. As soon as I arrived, I thought, what a beautiful state! Charlotte was a growing city, with lush spring flowers everywhere, and a very cosmopolitan flavor. It was a very busy, thriving city, and I loved the Southern accent everyone had!

If one wanted to stay in for dinner, the Charlotte Regional Farmers Market had all the ingredients for a wonderful dinner. There was lots of produce, of course, and on Saturdays, you could find wine for sale as well as delicious pastry, and even some free samples!

If you wanted to go out for dinner or entertainment, there were lots of awesome restaurants, and let's not forget the gorgeous, huge SouthPark Mall. I could spend the whole day there shopping. At night, people were out and about at restaurants, breweries, and nightclubs featuring live music and entertainment. Charlotte is home to the Carolina Panthers, as well as lots of other sports attractions, so when I had any free time away from work, I was definitely out on the town!

ATLANTA, GEORGIA

Atlanta was a bit different because the company had purchased a townhouse there that the employees were to stay in when working at the Atlanta HealthWays Centers. The townhouse had a full kitchen and lovely furnished rooms, so that I didn't have to go to restaurants unless I wanted to; I could cook my own meals right there. This was a nice change from all the other assignments I had around the country and I took full advantage of it. This isn't to say that I didn't do a lot of sightseeing! Underground Atlanta was one stop on my list. It is a shopping and entertainment district in downtown Atlanta, covering about six blocks with lots of shopping malls, restaurants, and live entertainment; a real tourist destination with over a hundred years of history.

The weather in Atlanta was always hot and humid when I was there, but the people were friendly and lots of fun. Traveling around Atlanta was easy to learn because the main highway wraps in a circular fashion all around the city, with exit and on-ramps all around.

There were nine HealthWays Family Medical Centers in Atlanta. I was stationed at the largest one, with staff from the other centers coming in for the system orientation training sessions.

I was also there when the Atlanta market initiated a new "Automated Call Distribution" telephone system that was shared by all the HealthWays Centers in the state. Patient calls were taken in the order they were received and directed to the appropriate location. The new telephone system helped the Patient Service Representatives manage their calls and provide quick customer service.

PENNSYLVANIA

My assignment in Pennsylvania was a different story. I flew in on a Sunday afternoon, deposited my luggage at the hotel, and decided to find the medical office where I would be teaching, since it was my first time there.

To give you some background, the insurance company I worked for had recently purchased this small chain of Family Medical Care Centers, and I had heard that the staff was very unhappy about this change. They were now required to learn a new computer system, and the center there was under new management.

I'm glad I listened to my intuition that this might be a difficult assignment, but I never expected what happened next! When I arrived at the center, it was about to close for the evening. I asked the receptionist, who was shutting down her computer for the night, where the training was going to be held the following day because I was the instructor. She directed me to a small conference room. What a mess it was when I walked in! All the computers were piled up in a corner, not on the tables. The tables were covered with remnants of paper cups, paper plates, and rotting leftover food scraps. Then the receptionist announced that she was leaving, but I was welcome to stay and lock up. "Good luck tomorrow," she said with a laugh.

There was no way I could conduct any kind of training in this room in its current state. So I had no choice but to stay, roll up my sleeves, and clean and set up the room. First I had to gather up all the trash, wash the tables down, set up all the computers in rows on the tables, and then hook them up to the network. I had to call the Help Desk back home for assistance. I think I left the center after midnight, exhausted and with no dinner. I dropped into bed at the hotel, not looking forward to the next day! But I was determined not to fail. Once again, I reminded myself of Miss Earhart's quote: "You can do anything you decide to do."

We had been assured that the conference room would be all set up for the training and that the computers were ready to go, but something had told me to double-check. I'm certainly glad I did! People can be so mean when they are not happy with a situation.

DALLAS, TEXAS

And then there was Dallas. Wow, gorgeous! The men there were gorgeous too, and such gentlemen. Everywhere I went, one of them would open the door for me, take off his cowboy hat, smile, and say, "Have a great day!" I felt as if I were in the movies. Every Texas man I met in the city wore a cowboy hat, exotic cowboy boots, and expensive-looking suits – very impressive.

As a woman, if you walk into a nice restaurant in Dallas and there's a cowboy sitting at your table, he will stand up until you are seated. I had to pinch myself. I could really get used to this!

Dallas had the beautiful and spacious Galleria Mall, with four levels of shopping, restaurants, an impressive ice rink, a theater, and signature shops from around the globe. I spent lots of time at the Galleria, since the hotel I was staying at was nearby. The only regret I had in Dallas was that I never got to see the Dallas Cowboys play; they are one of my favorite teams.

There were lots of other states I traveled to for work, but these are the ones that stand out the most in my mind.

READY FOR A CHANGE

Traveling for work as a single girl sounded very exciting when I started, but the glamour quickly wore off. Although I loved my job, after five years of constant travel, I was completely burned out. I had to pack five days' worth of suits, all my instructor notes, and any training material I could not ship ahead of time. Then I had to drag everything through miles of airports.

I certainly racked up the airline miles quickly, and was thrilled that I got to see so much of the U.S. in my job, enjoying how different each state was. But was it all worth it? The traveling was getting to be too much for me. I would fly out on a Sunday afternoon, teach all week, catch a red-eye flight back home on Friday night, spend the weekend washing clothes, paying bills, catching up with family and friends who usually wanted to go out to dinner, and then pack to leave Sunday afternoon for the next assignment. I didn't even enjoy dinners out much, because it's what I did all week when I was teaching on location!

CHAPTER 6

CREATIVITY

A NEW DIRECTION

It was time to get back to a normal life – not that I had ever known *normal* so far in my life. But a nine-to-five job with little to no travel suddenly sounded wonderful to me. I was ready for a change. I needed more structure in my life. I needed to settle down!

I returned home and thought about what I wanted to do going forward. I had loved designing the training materials. That was the best part of my previous job because it allowed me to be very creative. I decided I wanted to move on from facilitating classes to designing them.

I became an Instructional Designer, working with instructors and subject matter experts to identify client training needs and then create PowerPoint presentations, develop study guides, training videos, job aids, animation, and training infographics for clients.

Throughout the course of my career, I have taken numerous ASTD (American Society for Training and Development) courses, attended various training webinars, as well as Langevin Learning Services workshops, earning certificates in Instructional Design and Education Project Management to expand my skills. It was always exciting to learn new design methods and techniques in my field.

Today, I am still enjoying what I do as a Senior Instructional Designer and am always looking for new ways of developing training materials. I build instructor-led classes using a blended-learning approach; interactive classroom learning, demonstrations, hands-on student exercises, animated videos, as well as creating knowledge assessments. I strive to ensure that the classes are interesting and informative for all the participants.

MY HOUSE

Once I was settled into my career, I decided I wanted to own my own house. Dad helped me find the perfect place: a small Cape-style house with lots of land. It was like my own miniature farm! Yes, it needed work, but that was perfect because it gave me a purpose, a project I desperately needed in my life. I didn't mind pouring whatever extra money I had into it and enlisting Mom and Dad's help – especially Dad. The house was mine and no one could take it away! Dad was a miracle worker. He could fix anything, and turned my fixer-upper into a lovely home. It also gave me more time to spend with him, helping him with whatever I could.

We had ourselves a full house remodeling project to complete. Dad and I took down old wallpaper in many of the rooms, and painted the walls in soft pastel colors. Dad put in a beautiful new steel-insulated front door for me that didn't let the cold in, as the old wooden door had.

I had every window in the house replaced with modern insulated vinyl windows, and then I hung curtains in every room. Although I had to replace a few appliances, it was well worth it for the new conveniences that modern appliances offer. Dad even helped me pick out furniture for a few of the rooms in my house. Slowly, my tiny fixer-upper transformed into a showpiece, at least to me. I loved my house!

On weekend evenings, Dad would often stop by just to say, "Hi. Do you have some time for your old man?" We would sit outside on my small deck and talk. He would ask for a glass of soda, but instruct me not to tell Mom. Lately Dad's health had been starting to deteriorate. He was on a lot of medications, a restricted diet, and it was getting harder for him to walk, but he never missed his weekly visits to me. This is one of my fondest memories of him!

DECORATING

I found that I really enjoyed decorating my house for the holidays and creating new flower gardens every spring. It was fun to fill the deck with planters of growing vegetables, too. I also planted different kinds of herbs in small containers on my deck and then used them in food recipes.

Occasionally I dried parsley or basil, shredding them and placing them in their designated spice rack jars to use when needed. Fresh-cut chives from my garden were delicious on baked potatoes and I even cut mint leaves to sweeten my tea. These are all techniques I learned from my grandfather on the farm as a child.

I loved to decorate the house during the holidays. Yes, I know that it is so much easier (and cheaper) to let the home space always look the same. However, some of us love change, as crazy as that may sound. There's Christmas, of course, with candles in the windows, Santas and snowmen everywhere, twinkling snow and hot chocolate by the fire. Most people stop right there, but then comes St. Patrick's Day, Easter, the Fourth of July, Halloween, and Thanksgiving, to mention a few.

I guess that decorating is a passion and a chance for creativity for me. Certainly the boxes of decorations pile up and attic space gets limited, but I wouldn't have it any other way!

CRAFTS

Because I loved being creative, and I now knew how to sew, I decided to make children's themed pillows and sell them at crafts fairs for extra money.

Once I had three sides of a pillow sewn, I filled the inside with soft fiberfill and then sewed up the remaining side. Each one turned out so beautiful.

It was so much fun watching the children grab for the pillow with their favorite character on it and beg their mother to buy it for them.

I really enjoyed the atmosphere of the crafts shows and viewing all the lovely handiwork of the various artists exhibiting. Very inspiring!

People seemed to love my handmade pillows, so I started creating some sports-related pillows for the adults. I also designed fancy gift baskets to sell.

My crafts business was becoming very successful, and I was always thinking of new ways to advertise or to add to my product line.

I added some holiday-themed craft items to my shows, usually depending on the season. Of course, most of them were Halloween or Christmas-related, which people seemed to love!

THE SALESMAN

In my search for new craft ideas to implement, I stumbled across "the Salesman." He was a five-foot-tall, smiling scarecrow for sale in a local boutique. He was gorgeous! I purchased him and brought him to all my craft shows. He was quite a hit with all the customers. Everyone wanted to buy him, but I told them, "He's my Salesman. I can't sell him." I know people came to my booth because he stood out. It didn't hurt that his presence also helped me sell more items!

And as an added bonus, "The Salesman" fit in perfectly with my fall decorations at the house!

As I said earlier, when I love someone or something, I give it a name. The Salesman will always be a part of my permanent craft table display.

CREATING PORCELAIN DOLLS

I have always loved my dolls. When a friend told me about porcelain doll classes, it sounded so interesting that I signed up right away. Each week I would go to class and after attending for three years, and learning a great deal along the way, I became somewhat proficient at the process.

In my class, each student would choose a doll to create. The process started with cleaning raw, soft clay molds of all the doll's body parts. These molds were hollow, so great care had to be taken in the cleaning and polishing process, using special tools. After the doll's parts were cleaned, the instructor fired them in a kiln. Once fired, the molds couldn't break unless dropped on the floor.

As the process continued, the doll was gently pieced together and fired in the kiln once more. After that, the fun part began; using various China paints to color in the doll's eyes, lips, nails, eyebrows, and skin tone. Then, once again, the color was fired in to become permanent. Once the doll was assembled, it was time to decide how to dress it, and purchase the appropriate material to make the clothing.

Our teacher worked with a talented seamstress who created tiny doll clothing items for the students' dolls. We would pick out and purchase material of our choice at the fabric store, in line with the style for the clothing we had chosen and dependent on the type of doll we were making – a fashion doll, a baby doll, a young girl or boy doll, or an angel fig-ure. A couple of weeks later, we would receive the finished piece of clothing. I also purchased a wig and shoes for my doll.

Porcelain doll making is a long and expensive pro-cess, but it is an art form, and the results can be magnificent!

Here is a picture of what I consider my best creation. I am very proud to say I made her myself! She is about fifteen inches tall and took me quite a few months to complete.

CHAPTER 7

FRIENDS & FAMILY

FRIENDS

My friends have always been very important to me. One can say that friends are like chocolate – you can never have enough. Some are better for you than others – like dark chocolate! But in reality, there are only a few people you can call *true* friends; the rest are acquaintances. Not that there is anything wrong with acquaintances! But there is a special bond, an unknown attachment, even a melding of the minds on occasion, that doesn't happen with acquaintances.

> **"A true friend is someone who thinks that you're a good egg even though he knows that you are slightly cracked."**
> **—Bernard Meltzer**

PLAYING POOL

One of my good friends, Jeanie, whom I had known since college and my Burlingame days, had recently gotten divorced. Now that I was back home, she wanted me to start going out on weekends with her to find new friends. We did go to some nightclubs, but the crowds weren't our cup of tea, so we had to think of other ways to "meet men," as she put it.

There was a class at the local community college: "Learn To Play Pool!" So we signed up and found out that we both really enjoyed the game. Armed with our newfound expertise in the game, we joined a local pool club and started playing in their league once a week in the evenings. I have to say it wasn't as easy as it looked – pool is a game of skill and chance. We definitely needed more skill and kept our fingers crossed for chances!

In my third year of playing on the league with the same team, we won a trophy – so exciting! I even got a patch that year for a "9 On The Snap." I put the patch into a picture frame so that I could marvel at my accomplishment, knowing it was probably a fluke and that I would never get another one again. But it was so much fun!

Jean and I always greatly enjoyed playing pool on the league. That's where I drank my first beer, because it's what almost everyone drank at the pool club. But it tended to make me need to pee all the time and I really didn't enjoy it, so I stopped ordering it.

TWO HOPEWELL

Sometimes Jeanie and I would go out just to listen to a good band and dance. That's how I met the gang from Two Hopewell. Every Sunday night there was a group of five women who would meet there in the downstairs lounge area and hang out. Two Hopewell was a real upscale restaurant with delicious food; a comfortable, classy place with a great disc jockey in the restaurant's downstairs lounge area every Sunday night who played the best songs. We all laughed, danced, and basically had a great time. There was no pressure to meet men. We were just a group of women enjoying ourselves and having a great time together. The crowd was about our age, with professional jobs and attitudes. I felt that I fit in perfectly, and started making my Sunday evenings "Two Hopewell evenings."

Gail was one of the girls at Two Hopewell. She was this tall, beautiful, blonde-haired, friendly person who asked me to join their table of women. She and I hit it off immediately – like sisters. We both had the same interests and tastes. She quickly became my best friend.

Although I don't travel for work very often now, Gail still does, so we try to get together for dinner or a show every few weeks or whenever we can, to catch up. Gail has the coolest (and very spry) ninety-plus-year-old mom, whom she takes care of. She also has a very busy work schedule managing a department. I don't know how she does it all. So it's a real treat for me when she's available for a girls' night out!

> **"A man is what he is. Weak or strong, ugly or handsome. But a woman is who she wants to be - sweet or bittersweet, quiet or vibrant, cool and removed, or warm and sensuous. Her beauty is hers to create."**
> **—Unknown**

"THEME" NIGHTS

The owner of the restaurant, Nell, was also about our age, although her husband was older. Nell wanted to bring more people into her restaurant; not just for the food, but also for her Sunday night gatherings in the lounge downstairs. She asked our group for ideas and that's how the idea for a different theme night every Sunday evening came to be.

Nell started advertising in the local newspaper about the Sunday night Theme Nights and wouldn't you know, it turned out to be a great success! Lots of new faces started to show up on Sunday evenings and the place was always packed.

Everyone had to dress for the theme of the week if they wanted to come into the lounge on Sunday evenings. Wow, that was an awesome year with great, clean fun! When the weather was nice, we'd hang out in the restaurant's outside bar area, an enclosure engulfed in twinkling lights, a large fire pit in the center lit up with a crackling fire, surrounded by chairs all around, and of course great music. So much fun!

FLOWER POWER

My favorite Theme Night of all was the Sixties Night. We had so much fun seeing everyone dressed up in sixties and seventies style clothing!

Here are some of the symbols of this generation:
Miniskirts and paisley shirts
Long hair and maxi skirts
Muscle cars and Motown songs
Peace and love all around
College campuses were the scene
Psychedelic – everywhere and in between
Vietnam, inflation, Civil Rights
Bell bottoms and peasant tops
Woodstock and Ashbury Park.

And let's not forget these:
Flowers, freedom, "Make love, not war," Haight-Ashbury, tie-dye, bell bottoms, sandals, folk songs, vinyl records, Woodstock, love-ins, VWs.

"All you need is love."
—The Beatles

"WILD WEST"

We also had a "Wild West" Theme Night on Sunday night at Two Hopewell. It was a great time and we all looked forward to the weekends!

"MARDI GRAS"

The "Mardi Gras" Night was another big hit, with everyone dressed up in beads and masks.

"IN HOLLYWOOD"

For the fabulous "In Hollywood" Theme Night, we all got all dressed up as our favorite celebrity. So much fun!

There were many other wonderful events at Two Hopewell, including a fantastic New Year's Eve celebration that no one wanted to miss!

OUR FIRST DATE

My friendship with Gail continued, and has to this day. She is my sister in every way but biological. My best friend! And it was through Gail that I met a wonderful, smart gentleman. He's so much like my dad, it's amazing! Although he was never a pilot, he can fix anything, just like my dad, and has the same wonderful personality. His name is Ken and he is handsome, tall, loving, and my best friend. He's perfect for me and I love him very much.

And to think that I almost blew it on our first date! The plan was to meet him at an upscale outdoor shopping center in town at 11:00 a.m. on a Sunday morning. "Dress casual and we'll take a ride down to the shoreline," he said. Of course, it took me a long time to decide what to wear. I was a bit nervous and wanted to look my best. I changed outfits a few times before deciding on the perfect casual capris, top, and sandals to wear. I was so focused on getting ready that I forgot the time, and there was something

I needed to do before meeting Ken because I didn't know what time we would be getting back to town.

It was Father's Day and I HAD to visit my dad's grave. I never missed stopping by the cemetery on a holiday or his birthday. It was very important to me to put flowers at the gravesite for Father's Day for him. Needless to say, I hit lots of traffic and was about forty minutes late for my first date with Ken. Isn't that always the way when you're in a hurry? I felt so bad, thinking surely he'd be gone by the time I arrived, but there he was, standing on the spot!

WOW! was all I could think of. He waited for me! He was gorgeous! I had to apologize and explain myself. He didn't even complain. He said, "I thought something had happened to you." What a nice guy! He drove us down to the shoreline as promised and we walked on the beach for hours. We talked and got to know each other. Ken was so interesting, with a wonderful sense of humor. He was the perfect gentleman, too! The day flew by like magic. And then he asked if I could stay and have dinner with him at Cherrystones Restaurant in Old Lyme, Connecticut. We had a wonderful dinner and continued talking till it was dark outside. Then Ken drove me back to my car at the shopping center in town and said he'd like to see me again. Of course I said yes. Amazingly, I already felt safe and secure with him, as if I had known him forever. And that is how the story of our wonderful romance began.

MY SOULMATE

As our relationship continued and I got to know Ken more and more, I realized that he was the nicest, sweetest guy I had ever met. He often bought me beautiful roses for no reason. He would say, "I like to see you smile. I know that you love flowers."

I found out that Ken was also into crafts just as I was, and he was making beautiful stained glass treasures, like stained glass decorative mirrors, business card holders and night-lights. He also designed lighted bottles for sale.

Ken would occasionally surprise me with a gift of one of his stained glass creations. One of my favorites, which I have hung up in my bedroom, is a stained glass tulip in a frame. Gorgeous!

In time, we merged our talents and products into one business. Today I really enjoy working with him on our various craft projects, and we are always looking for new ideas to develop together.

SYNCHRONICITY

I had always said that I wanted to marry someone like my dad. Ken is a kind, good-hearted person, like he was. And he always puts his arm around me, just like my dad did with my mom. I only wish that Ken had had a chance to meet my dad before he died. I know they would have been such good friends.

I am so grateful that Ken and I met and that we still continue to share many adventures and wonderful memories together. I often think about our first date and how it could have turned out so differently for me if he hadn't waited.

You might think this is crazy, but I think my dad brought Ken to me. To find a soul mate so much like my father would be quite a coincidence. But as Deepak Chopra writes in his 2003 book, *The Spontaneous Fulfillment of Desire*, "There are no coincidences in this world; only Synchronicity. Coincidences are no accidents but rather signals from the universe which can guide us towards our true destiny."

ROXIE

We are now blessed with Roxie, our beautiful dove-gray Weimaraner. The Weimaraner is a large dog that was originally bred for hunting in the early nineteenth century in Europe. Weimaraners were used by royalty for hunting large game such as boar, bear and deer.

Roxie is a sweet, gentle giant of a dog that loves my three cats. She often gives them wet kisses on their foreheads. I actually think that Roxie believes that she is a cat too, albeit a rather large one at that, because she always licks her paws clean. When Roxie is happy, she shows it with her ears. Her long, floppy ears kind of round out away from her head, and her little stick of a tail beats so fast. She even dances around in circles when Kenny walks through the door each evening after work. So cute!

CHAPTER 8

REFLECTIONS OF MY LIFE

LOOKING BACK

It has now been many years since my marriage to Ralph ended. Today life is much calmer for me, and I am at peace with the sadness of the past. I am also so grateful for the wonderful support from my friends.

Looking back, I see that having had to grow up so quickly and deal with an extraordinary set of circumstances most people could never imagine or relate to, or even understand how to react in such a situation, I did my best and now I am stronger for it. I see life differently. I respect individuality and try not to judge. Unless you are in another person's shoes, you can never truly understand or judge another human being for their actions.

As a child, daily life was hard work on the farm, and I thought that when I grew up, life would be different. I would meet my Prince Charming and live happily ever after. But no one knows what detours life will give you or what's coming down the pike for us, regardless of age, wealth, or power.

LIFE THOUGHTS

With all the millions of people in the world it seems that there only a few that touch our core, and as we grow older, it seems that our world gets smaller. For example, the neighborhood park we loved to play in as a child seemed so large and full of fun activities to get involved in. Today, as an adult, that same park seems so small.

LIFE

Life is a series of opportunities and tests (usually more tests than opportunities). But I believe that when opportunity comes around, one should seize it. Take the challenge, take the risk. It's better than wondering "what if"!

ON GETTING OLD

As a friend of mine likes to say; "Getting old is not for sissies." And it is so true… one day your hair is dark and you want it to be lighter. The next day, it seems, your hair is turning gray, and you want it to be darker again.

When you're young, you play hard and if you fall, no problem… you just get up and start over. When you're older, if you fall, you hope that you can get up and start again!

It is exciting to get colored contacts and change your eye color when you are young. Not so much when you HAVE to put on glasses or contacts to be able to drive, or read a newspaper. And those wonderful, sexy four-inch heels – a must for nightclubbing. But the curse of the bunions can reduce you to flats. Lately the washer is shrinking all my clothes. I don't eat any more than I used to. Time to buy a new washer and stop all this craziness!

PARENTS

When we were small we wanted to be on our own. When we got older we wanted them to be our friends and be "cool." Now, I just wish they were still around!

MOM & DAD'S FIFTIETH WEDDING ANNIVERSARY

My parents were married for over fifty years before they died. Gosh, I can't even imagine! They were always so happy and did everything together. I felt so lucky to have them together, especially since I had a lot of friends whose parents were divorced.

For their fiftieth wedding anniversary, my brother and I threw them a surprise dinner party at an exclusive restaurant and banquet facility, and invited all their friends. There must have been seventy people at least who came to celebrate with us. How we ever got away with surprising Mom and Dad I'll never know, but I do know they were so thrilled!

The day was perfect and the food and decorations were fabulous. I ordered a huge anniversary cake for them, complete with buttercream frosting and fancy gold lettering, and placed it on the table next to a framed picture of their wedding day. We all took pictures as they cut the first piece of cake together. We even commissioned a piano player to play their favorite songs during dinner. I know Mom and Dad had the best time, and I am so glad that we had a chance to do this for them.

ANGELS

My dad once told me that he saw an angel when he was a child and it was amazing! I have never seen an angel, but once when I really needed my guardian angel, I heard him speak to me. Now my dad is an angel. I wish I could see him!

I believe that all the people who have touched my heart and now are gone are my guardian angels. I know they are near and will always be close by when needed.

HEROES

I learned that our heroes are just as vulnerable as we are when my mom was diagnosed with cancer. It was a sad lesson. We cannot fill ourselves with questions like, "Why did this happen?" but rather ask ourselves, "How can we best deal with what life has dished out?" Admittedly, the mind suffers as much as the body and our heroes are becoming fewer and fewer, but we must maintain a positive attitude to survive.

CHALLENGES

I've realized that a good challenge brings out my competitive spirit. We are only as old as we feel. It is important to stay challenged throughout life. I am a proud baby boomer. My generation never accepted what was before us; we questioned everything. For most of us, this thinking instilled a way of life. Many fifty and sixty-year-olds today are not anticipating their retirement just yet, but rather what new project or career to tackle next.

"Do not go gently into that good night."
—Dylan Thomas

TIME

Time goes fast, time goes slow

It never seems to go the way you want it to go.

Late for this, early for that

On time is a far harder act!

—Me

> **"Life isn't about waiting for the storm to pass... it is about learning to dance in the rain."**
> **—Vivian Green**

FAREWELL TO TENNIS

They say that tennis is a mind game; mental toughness is key! But so is physical agility and flexibility. As one ages, the mind stays strong, but the body weakens. You go from playing singles to doubles, and then to just watching the game on TV.

As I hang up my tennis racquet, I thank the players that increased my love of the game by their prowess and quick thinking. Here's hats off to my best opponents (a.k.a friends).

COINCIDENCES

Long ago, I found out there are no coincidences in life. There are many things and events that are unexplainable. When someone very close to you dies, I believe they want to communicate, and they will find small ways of doing so.

BIRDS

Birds are sent from the Spirit. My favorite is the hawk. I see it often, in the daytime and the evening – or maybe it just has a big family! They say that hawks help you ride the winds of change... I don't know, but I admire their grace and beauty.

Doves are special too. When my mother died and joined my father, I saw two doves walk slowly across the cemetery road together. Was it a sign? I want to believe it was – and they were telling me that they are reunited and at peace.

"Everything is possible for him who believes."
—Mark 9:23

PEACE

Now I pray for peace worldwide; too many wars and too many sons and daughters lost (physically or otherwise) in too many places around the globe.

LIFE IS A GIFT

The lessons we learn in life are nothing if we do not act on them. Become a better person with that knowledge! My being, my style, has developed from being pushed into adulthood, often not willingly. I've learned that life is what you make of it. It is important to feel with your heart, to love, to remember those who have touched our hearts, to share, and to never fear being alone. Life is a gift and a composite of the wisdom gained along the way.

"The only person you are destined to become is the person you decide to be."

—Ralph Waldo Emerson

WE

We work to play
We practice to win
We read so we can know
We cook so we can eat
We travel so we can see
We listen so we can hear
We learn so we can master
We open our hearts so we can love
We touch so we can feel
And we teach so others can learn too.
—Me

ACKNOWLEDGEMENTS

To Gail W., my sister in every way but biological! Thank you for all your support and guidance in the creation and development of this book. You, an accomplished writer yourself, made the process so much easier for me with your wonderful tips and ideas. Thank you again! I couldn't have done this without you.

To my editor, Nina, I am so thrilled that you accepted the job of editing my manuscript! Your professionalism and wonderful comments and ideas have truly raised my book to the next level. I have enjoyed working with you tremendously.

To Ken, my rock and dearest partner in life, thank you for being by my side every step of the way, and for encouraging me to dig deeper all the time.

To my readers, thank you for reading my book. I hope you have enjoyed it and that it helped you reflect on the powerful, often painful events in your own lives that have shaped who you are today. May you too find peace and happiness in your life.

CPSIA information can be obtained
at www.ICGtesting.com
Printed in the USA
LVHW010843040820
662306LV00011B/686